Let's get moving
Up a Mountain

Emma Lynch

Heinemann
LIBRARY

Little Nippers

www.heinemann.co.uk/library
Visit our website to find out more information about **Heinemann Library** books.

To order:
☎ Phone 44 (0) 1865 888066
📄 Send a fax to 44 (0) 1865 314091
💻 Visit the Heinemann Bookshop at www.heinemann.co.uk/library to browse our catalogue and order online.

First published in Great Britain by Heinemann Library, Halley Court, Jordan Hill, Oxford OX2 8EJ, part of Harcourt Education.
Heinemann is a registered trademark of Harcourt Education Ltd.

Editorial: Jilly Attwood and Kate Bellamy
Design: Jo Hinton-Malivoire
Models made by: Jo Brooker
Picture Research: Rosie Garai and Emma Lynch
Production: Séverine Ribierre

Originated by Dot Gradations
Printed and bound in China by South China Printing Company

ISBN 0 431 16480 0 (hardback)
08 07 06 05 04
10 9 8 7 6 5 4 3 2 1

ISBN 0 431 16485 1 (paperback)
08 07 06 05 04
10 9 8 7 6 5 4 3 2 1

British Library Cataloguing in Publication Data
Lynch, Emma
Let's get moving... up a mountain
591.5'09143
A full catalogue record for this book is available from the British Library.

Acknowledgements
The publishers would like to thank the following for permission to reproduce photographs:
Corbis/Royalty Free pp. **4a**, **5a**, **6a**, **7a**, **9**, **10a**, **13**, **14a**, **15a**, **16a**, **16b**, **19a**, **20a**, **21a**; Getty Images p. **18** (Photodisc); Harcourt Education Ltd pp. **4b**, **5b**, **6b**, **7b**, **8b**, **10b**, **11b**, **12**, **14b**, **15b**, **17**, **18b**, **19b**, **20b**, **21b**, **22** (Tudor Photography); NHPA p. **23** (Derek Karp).

Cover photograph reproduced with permission of Alamy Images/Stock Connection Inc.

Our thanks to Annie Davy for her assistance in the preparation of this book.

2

Contents

At the bottom

peak

Reach up high to the sky like a mountain peak.

4

Sway in the breeze like the mountain trees.

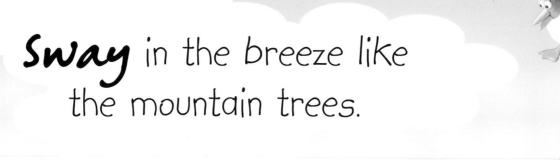

Along the stream

Run like a wolf on the scent of a meal.

Walk like a dipper along the mountain stream.

Climbing

Climb like a salmon
fighting its way upstream.

Kick your legs out
and hop like a hare.

Grrrrooowwwww!!!

Stand up straight
and growl like
a bear.

Mountain range

Gallop like wild horses over the mountain range.

Faster, faster, then slow down again.

Over the rocks

Prowl like a mountain lion looking for some lunch.

Mooch like a moose who is on the loose.

antlers

Near the top

Spring from rock to rock
like a mountain goat.

spring

Over the mountain

Spread like
the snow
over the
rocks below.

Soar like an eagle
over the icy peaks.

Tumbling down

Roll down towards the ground
like the leaves from the trees.

Tumble like a waterfall into the mountain stream.

whoosh!

Rest

Even beavers get tired, so
sit down and have a rest.

Come back soon for
 another mountain trek!

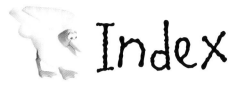

Index

The end

Notes for adults

Let's get moving! explores the many different ways humans can move and encourages children to take part in physical activity. *Let's get moving!* also supports children's growing knowledge and understanding of the wider world, introducing them to different plants and animals and the way they move and grow. Used together, the books will enable comparison of different movements and of a variety of habitats and the animals that live in them.

The key curriculum Early Learning Goals relevant to this series are:

Early Learning Goals for movement
• Move with confidence, imagination and in safety
• Move with control and coordination

Early Learning Goals for sense of space
• Show awareness of space, self and of others

Early Learning Goals for exploration and investigation
• Find out about and identify some features of living things

This book introduces the reader to a range of movements used by animals that live up a mountain. The book will also help children extend their vocabulary as they hear new words like *peak*, *range*, *mane* and *antlers*. You may like to introduce and explain other new words yourself, like *valley*, *habitat* and *glacier*.

Additional information

Most living things can move. Humans and many other animals have skeletons and muscles to support and protect their bodies and to help them move. Mount Everest is the highest peak in the world at 8,850 metres above sea level. It is located on the borders of China and India. The difference between a mountain and a hill is that a mountain has a greater height and volume. A volcano is a type of mountain.

Follow-up activities

• Can the children think of other mountain animals? Try to copy their movements.
• How else can the children move their bodies? How many different ways can they come up with and when do they use these movements?
• Draw or paint the different plants and animals that live up a mountain to make a wall display.